I0054065

INCREASE

ON THE SUDDEN

SWING TRADING THE FOREX

A MECHANICAL TRADING SYSTEM
TO START WINNING TOMORROW

J.D. HYTER

Increase On the Sudden: Swing Trading the Forex

Copyright © 2024. J.D. Hyter

All rights reserved. No part of this publication may be reproduced, distributed, or transmitted in any form or by any means, including photocopying, recording, or other electronic or mechanical methods, without the prior written permission of the copyright holder, except in the case of brief quotations embodied in critical reviews and certain other noncommercial uses permitted by copyright law.

Book Design by
Transcendent Publishing

ISBN: 979-8-9900956-2-5

Forex trading contains substantial risk and is not for every investor. An investor could potentially lose all or more than the initial investment. Risk capital is money that can be lost without jeopardizing ones' financial security or life style. Only risk capital should be used for trading and only those with sufficient risk capital should consider trading. Past performance is not necessarily indicative of future results.

Printed in the United States of America.

DEDICATION

I dedicate this book to my father. Fifteen years ago, he assigned me the task of learning how to trade the Foreign Exchange market. He wanted to leave an inheritance to his children but he did not have the time to learn the trade, so he gave me all the resources needed to learn. My family, I, and now thousands of others are forever grateful!

Marvel not at the works of sinners; but trust in Yahuah, and abide in your labor: for it is an easy thing In the sight of Yahuah **on the sudden** to make a poor man rich.

Sirach 11:21

TABLE OF CONTEXT

If my goal is to provide for only myself that's **SELFISH**

If my goal is to provide for my wife that's **ADMIRABLE**

If my goal is to provide for my family that's **HONORABLE**

If my goal is to provide for STRANGERS that's **REMARKABLE!**

—J.D. HYTER

INTRODUCTION

Countless people scour the internet each year to find information on how to trade the financial markets. Reports will tell you that 90% of them come to failure within their first three months of trading.

Many spend thousands of dollars buying expensive coaching sessions and blowing out trading accounts. Some people have spent over a decade trying to become a profitable trader but have never had a profitable month.

Every so often, though, you hear about someone who began trading a few months ago and is doubling and tripling their trading accounts every quarter. What's the difference between the thousands losing and the very few who seem to be able to make money at will?

The difference is the struggling trader has common trading knowledge. Common trading knowledge is all over the internet for *free*. Unfortunately, most traders that are on the struggle bus are practicing the craft with common trading knowledge.

Common trading knowledge is the knowledge that big money institutions put out into the industry to trap the uninformed. They do this so they can turn you into a market donator. They teach you support and resistance, pivot points, and break-out trading strategies. They tell you where to place your stop loss, so they can push prices into that area to knock you out of your trade positions. Again, turning you into a market donator.

This book holds the answers you seek. When you remove all the industry indicators from your trading chart, you will begin to truly see the market. What you need is to acquire the ability and hard skill to read a price chart.

Some people are lucky to have been taught how to read a price chart from the beginning of their trading careers. Others stay on the struggle bus because they don't understand that the real trading skill is the ability to read a price chart. I truly believe this book will open your eyes to how the market really works and moves.

The key to the trading kingdom is summed up in two words: MARKET CYCLE. If you learn this one piece of trading knowledge, you will exit the struggle bus and begin the lucrative journey of becoming a profitable trader.

WHAT IS PRICE ACTION?

Price action refers to the movement of a financial asset's price displayed on a price chart over a given period of time. It reveals crucial information about market sentiment and the behavior of market participants. Understanding price action is essential for any trader looking to make informed decisions. The beauty of price action is that it's based on human behavior and humans are habitual creatures.

With that being the case, a trader can learn daily patterns and setups that consistently win in the financial markets. What I am trying to tell you is that you can learn how to track prices to the point that you will be able to predict what the market is most probable to do next.

This gives chart readers an unfair advantage in the marketplace. Smart traders describe it as a hunter tracking his prey. When you understand how the market moves you can wait patiently for the perfect trading opportunity.

Pure price action trading uses almost zero indicators. Indicators are also called lagging indicators, which means that they lag behind the current market conditions. Thousands of would-be traders do not understand that they are losing in large part because they are using lagging indicators.

By the time most indicators give you a go signal, the best price movements are over. In comparison, a trader who reads the price action will be in the market at the start of the best price movements. Timing is vital when you are doing any type of trading. The lower the time frame you trade on, the more accurate your timing needs to be.

This book will cover the best price action swing trade you can take. You will learn how to track market prices and then take advantage of the repeat patterns that print to the charts. It has been said amongst the elite traders of the world that price action is KING.

I believe that to be true.

I struggled for years as a trader until I learned how to read the price action. When you remove all the indicators and just learn how to read a price chart, trading becomes much easier.

THE MARKET CYCLE

The world is full of cycles. There are agricultural cycles, seasonal cycles, planetary cycles, and the list goes on and on. The financial markets also have cycles that can be predicted.

The real power of chart reading is that market prices move in a trackable cycle.

Here is the basic market cycle. **TREND, TREND BREAK, RESTEST TO A NEW HIGH OR LOW**. That is the market cycle for all price charts. With study and observation, you will begin to see this market cycle take place every day in any asset class you study. The reason for this is that all markets are composed of human behavior. The bars that print on a price chart are the representation of humans making decisions.

The image below represents the majority of market participants buying the same asset at the same time, which causes its price to go up in value. We call this an Uptrend. The second image is when the majority sells an asset, causing the price to decrease. We call that a Downtrend.

UPTREND MARKET CYCLE

DOWNTREND MARKET CYCLE

The part that confuses people is that the market will sometimes go into a range cycle after the trending market cycle. So many traders have difficulty reading and understanding what's happening. Just consider a range a pause or half-time of the trending market cycle.

A range can last a long time in some cases. Bitcoin, for example, loves to range for weeks and then just take off like a rocket for a few days. A range is when prices are trapped and bouncing between two price points.

RANGING MARKET

Once you can read a price chart and see the market cycle, you now have the power to trade with uncanny accuracy. If you know that the market cycle has had a trend and a trend break. You now know that the **retest is next,** and you can trade that part of the market cycle with confidence. That is the swing in swing trading.

To easily see the market cycle in action, add a 21 exponential moving average to your price chart. Each picture example shown has the 21 exponential moving average added. If prices stay above the 21 exponential moving average, you are in an **uptrend**. Once prices break and close under the 21 exponential moving average, that is a **trend break**. When the price surges back above the 21 exponential moving average, it is attempting a **retest to a new high**. The same cycle happens in reverse for a downtrend market.

You will know that the market is in a ranging cycle when the 21 exponential moving average is moving sideways, resembling a rollercoaster.

You can simply add the moving average to any price chart to learn how to spot the market cycle. After you gain adequate chart hours by watching the 21 E.M.A, you will be able to SEE the market cycle. It has always been there but it takes a trained eye to see it.

THE RULE OF TWO

The market cycle is the high-level view of how market prices move on a candlestick price chart. If we drill down to a bar-by-bar situation, then you begin to see the **rule of two** in play. If you watch a price chart long enough, you will begin to see that the market moves in legs of two.

In the example from the last chapter, when you notice an **uptrend,** that price movement represents one leg. The **trend break** represents a correction in the market. Many times, this correction will have two legs back to and sometimes under the 21 EMA. The **retest to a new high** represents the second leg of the uptrend.

This is called the **rule of two**. When swing trading, a great strategy is to try to catch the second leg of a solid trend move. This strategy is so simple but also incredibly powerful. People want to make trading hard but, honestly, it's very easy if you keep things simple.

TREND LEG #2

TREND LEG #1

The rule of two can be seen all over a price chart if you know how to look for it. You can also see the rule of two inside very small trend moves. If you get three bars in a row in the same direction, then a break back to the 21 E.M.A., then another three bars move in the original direction, that's the **rule of two!**

Another word for the rule of two is called a measured move. If you measure a trend leg. You can expect to get a second leg that will be the same length or longer than the first. That is called a measured move. It's the rule of two; calling it a measured move is just another way to explain what is happening in the markets.

Once you understand and see the market cycle and the rule of two, you can begin to take some high-probability trades. It is hard to say why the market moves in twos. My best educated guess is that investment banks have large orders to fill every day.

Once they come into the market with a bundle of orders, they cause the market to move either up or down. Then counter trend traders see that first big move and mistakenly think it's over, and they place orders in the opposite direction, which causes the correction legs in the market.

Then the banks wait for prices to pull back so they can enter their second bundle of orders at a lower price. Once they enter that second time, we get the second leg in the rule of two and the market cycle. At this point, all traders that are trading now believe we are trending and place orders in the same direction, which causes the second leg to take off into a good strong trend.

If you trust in the rule of two and the market cycle, you will set yourself apart from the majority of day traders who lose. Understanding the rule of two is the essence of price chart reading.

FIBONACCI
RETRACEMENT ZONES

Fibonacci retracement zones are an essential aspect of technical analysis and our swing trading strategy. By identifying key levels based on Fibonacci ratios, we can anticipate where the second leg of a trend will begin. The Fibonacci technique is widely used across various financial markets, including stocks, forex, and cryptocurrencies.

I would say the Fibonacci tool is available on all trading platforms, but of course, I have not used every trading platform. I have yet to use any platform worth its weight that does not offer the Fibonacci retracement tool.

That alone is a clue of how valuable this tool is. When you spot a strong trend that looks to be pulling back, you can place a Fibonacci on it to see where the 50% - .618 zone is. That is where most normal trends will begin the second leg.

There are many different ratios that people use with this tool. I want to give you my settings because they are the settings that I used to earn 333% of my trading account balance in 27 days.

Here are my Fibonacci Settings.

0

0.124

0.236

0.382

0.5

0.618 - Golden Ratio

0.786

0.886

1

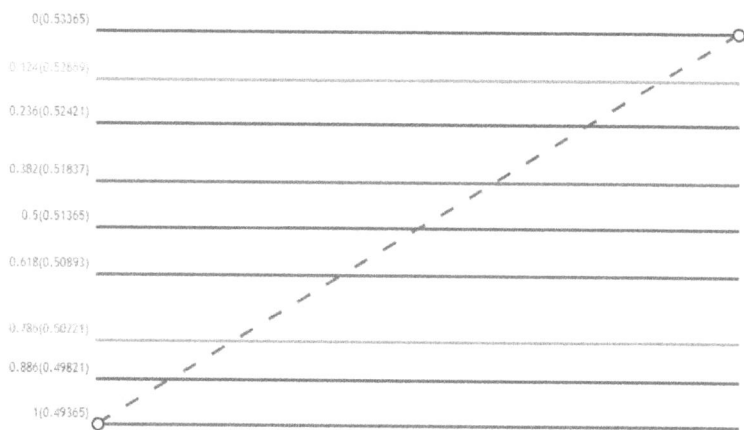

I will go deeper into how to use these settings to trade in the Forex 4-Hour Swing Trading Strategy section at the end of the book. Now let's look at how you can mathematically become one of the best traders in the world!

FORMULA TO BECOME A
PROFITABLE TRADER

There is a formula for becoming a profitable trader. It consists of three parts that work together to set you apart from the competition.

Strategy - The first thing you need is a trading strategy with at least a 1/1 risk-to-reward ratio that wins at 60%. The swing trading strategy I will lay out for you at the end of this book has consistently produced results of over 70%.

Risk - I suggest you risk 1% or less when you first begin trading. This is sound money management. If you were to somehow lose 10 trades in a row you are only down 10% in your trading account. When you first begin trading, the goal is to survive. You will survive by not risking too much of your account on any single trade. Always trade to be able to trade another day. Sometimes the markets are just too volatile for any strategy. Then, the next day, it's back to normal. Do not risk too much; one trade is not worth going out of business over.

Frequency - This is how many trades you will take each day, week, or month. It's hard to tell you how many to take. With this strategy, you have to trade when prices get to the entry zones. The more you look for solid trades, you will find the number that is good for your account size. Just try not to overtrade and enter too many positions at once for your account size.

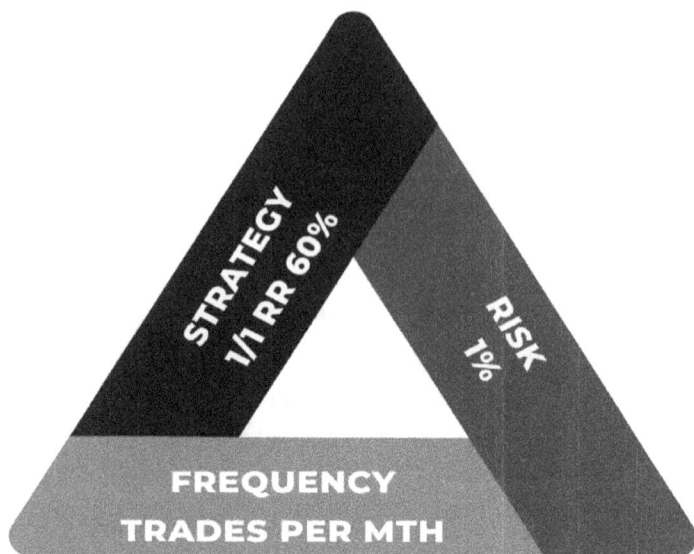

Now, with those three parts described, here is the formula.

Frequency * Strategy = Wins
Frequency - Wins = Losses
Wins - Losses = Net Wins
Net Wins * Risk = ROI

Let's plug some real numbers in so you can see how if you can win at just 60%, you will be one of the best traders in the world if you start with a $5,000 account.

100 * 60% = 60 wins
100 - 60 = 40 losses
60 - 40 = 20 net wins
20 * 1% = 20%
20% × 12 months = 240% a year

Twenty percent of $5,000 would be a profit of $1,000 in one month. That's $12,000 in one year. You could easily increase your profit by taking more trades or winning at a higher percentage than 60. Two things that can easily be done with the swing trading strategy you are about to learn.

These numbers are outstanding. You will not make a 240% return on your money doing anything else. If you leave that same $5,000 in a savings account, you would be lucky if you made $4.00 for the entire year.

FOREX 4-HOUR SWING TRADING STRATEGY

This strategy is so easy that you can start winning as soon as you start trading it. When I first saw this strategy, a tear ran down my face. After years of struggling, I could not believe that the answer to my trading woes was staring me in the face the whole time.

I had no idea about the market cycle, the rule of two, or the Fibonacci retracement tool. The crazy part is that they were there the whole time. Now that you have an understanding of how the market works, you can go to work and trade successfully.

Step 1 - Pick any asset you like. It really does not matter. This strategy works on any pair on a Japanese candlestick chart. Set your chart to the **4-HOUR** time frame. It also works on higher time frames, but I would not go to lower time frames.

Step 2 - Find a good trend leg that is beginning to have a pullback to the 21 EMA. If it's an uptrend, drag the Fibonacci tool from the bottom to the top of the trend. Your bottom Fibonacci number should be 1, and 0 should be at the top of the trend. If you are going short, the numbers will be reversed, with 1 at the top and 0 at the bottom.

Step 3 – Now, with the Fibonacci drawn on the chart, find the **0.5 - 0.618 zone**. We call it the 50% 618 zone or **SWEET SPOT!**

Place a rectangle in that area and make it some color you like. This zone is our entry zone. You can enter a trade anywhere in the zone. Some people like to enter as soon as prices touch the zone. Some like to set buy tops or sell tops to wait for prices to come out of the zone. That part is up to you; it's a trader's preference. Just remember that you are free to enter when you want once prices pull back to the **sweet spot**. Another area is the 0.618 mark that makes up the back end of the Sweet Spot. This area is called the **Golden Ratio**. Many traders love this area on a price chart. The **0.618** number has some mystic significance, but I have not studied enough about it to write about it. I will say prices tend to turn at this spot and begin the second leg.

Step 4 - Your stop loss goes below the **0.886 zone** on the Fibonacci, so do your math to risk only 1%.

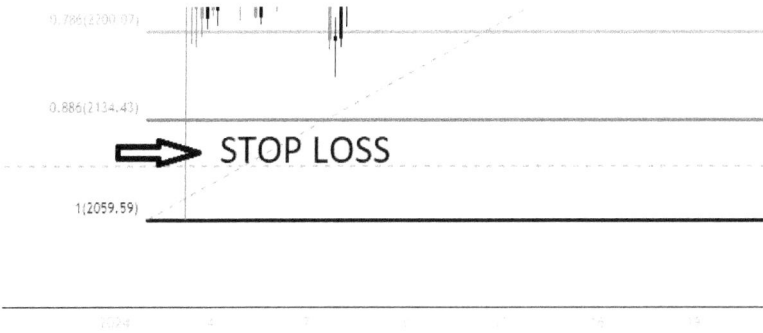

Step 5 - Now that you have the sweet spot, flip the Fibonacci tool and go from the opposite end that you just went from down to the **0.618** zone of the sweet spot. Now mark the sweet spot in the other direction and place another rectangle box in that zone. This is the Take Profit Box.

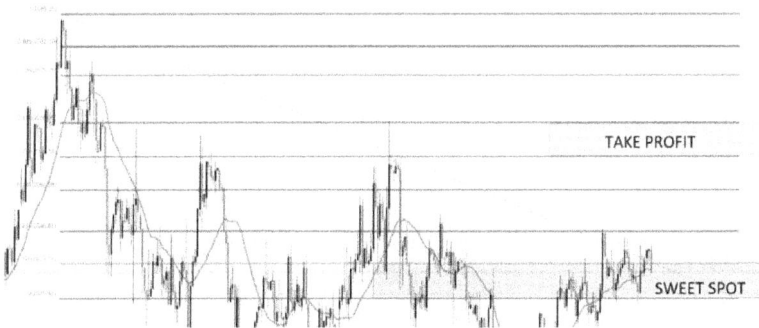

You can do this before you enter the trade to evaluate the risk-to-reward ratio. Many times, with this strategy, you will not have an exact 1/1 risk-to-reward ratio. The strategy wins at such a high rate, though, that it does not matter.

Step 6 - Now enter the trade; there is nothing else to do until prices reach the take profit zone. This mechanical strategy makes it great for new and struggling traders. You can only shoot yourself in the foot if you interfere with the trade. Learn to be disciplined and let the trade play out.

Step 7 - Once prices make it to the take profit zone, you have two options. You can close the trade out entirely and take the profit. Or you could take off half of your position and let the rest run. Just move to break even after you take off half. This is a trader's preference to how you want to manage the winning trade.

That's it. That's the strategy; put a bow on it. I know it may seem too simple to be true. That's the blessed part of this strategy. It really is this easy to make consistent profits in the markets. You will probably be tempted to make adjustments to this strategy; I wouldn't. I can only stand on what I have given you in this book. It has worked for me time and time again. Stick to 4-hour charts and stick to putting your stop under the 0.886 zone.

In the event that you lose a trade, do not despair; you only risked 1 %. Keep watching the market, looking for any sign of rejection. If the market starts moving back up abruptly, you can now enter again with a much better risk-to-reward ratio than the trade you lost. This time put your stop under the **1** zone. The profit target would remain the same. Now you have a shot at a very profitable trade, like a 1 to 5 or better risk to reward.

If you follow these steps, you will see instant positive results. The key is to implement this strategy in a trending market. This swing trading strategy is best used when markets are trending. If an asset has been in a range, do not try to put a Fibonacci on it. Look for a really good, strong trend leg. Trending markets are the conditions in which this strategy shines.

CONCLUSION

I f you are in total shock right now, that is normal. YES, profitable trading is this simple. To sum up this strategy, all we are doing is taking the **second leg of the market cycle**. The Fibonacci retracement tool gives us the exact area where prices are most likely to begin the second leg.

The 50% to .618 zone is considered the normal trend retracement area. The 32.8% zone is considered a strong trend. In this strategy, we are waiting for prices to reach the normal trend zone. We then take our profit before prices make it to an area that it had a hard time breaking through before.

Most traders do not know that investment banks, large hedge funds, and institutional traders are using automated trading robots to place their market orders. These automated bots are programmed with the premise of Fibonacci retracement zones.

So, what we are doing is trading with BIG money instead of trading against it. This strategy places you on the right side of the money wave 90% of the time, which moves you out of the 90% of losing traders category.

This is the secret sauce. You now have a swing trading strategy that you can begin to win with immediately. When I first learned this strategy, I did a 40-trade demo challenge and went 38 out of 40. Then, I tested again at 50 trades and went 45 out of 50.

I suggest that you also test on a demo account with paper money before you start to implement the strategy to build your confidence. Years of losing can definitely make you a skeptic. This swing trading strategy eliminates many factors that cause traders to lose.

You do not have to worry about what to do. The rules are set.

- Enter the market in the sweet spot; no signal candle is needed.
- Place your stop loss under the 0.886 Fibonacci line.
- Place a profit target box on the chart by flipping the Fibonacci and marking up the sweet spot in the other direction on the chart.
- Do not touch the trade until prices reach the take profit box.

Follow these simple rules and you will begin to win at a high rate. I personally like to take all my profit once we get to the take profit box. Many traders have great success taking off half their position because when you do catch a runner, that is a lot of extra cream. You now possess a proven winning trading strategy. All you need to do now is practice and look for trends showing correction pullback legs. Use the Fibonacci retracement tool and mark up your charts.

It's an easy thing to find three or four trades a day. You now possess secret trading knowledge to be able to **Increase on The Sudden!**

Thank you for purchasing this book. I pray it will empower you to finally cross over and become a profitable trader. Remember that simple is usually better, and swing trading is no different. In swing trading, keeping things simple is definitely better.

I wish you the best of luck and HAPPY TRADING!

GET MORE HELP

I f you want to see me implement this trading strategy, you can tune into my YouTube channel. I release a new swing trading chart lesson on Monday, Wednesdays, and Fridays at 10:00 AM EST www.youtube.com/@jdhyter

I also have a **Price Action Trading System** video course that takes you on a deep dive into how to apply price action trading with Fibonacci retracements in several other markets, such as the Binary Options market.

You can also join my **Swing Trading Titans Community,** where we post trade ideas that any member can take so you can earn while you learn. Both of these resources can be accessed on my website at:

www.jdhyter.com

Again, my name is J.D., and as always, I wish you…

Increase On The Sudden!

ABOUT THE AUTHOR

J.D. HYTER

|s a Swing Trader who created a unique trading system that combines pure Price Action trading with Fibonacci retracement zones. He currently trades in the Foreign Exchange markets, Binary Options markets, and Cryptocurrency markets.

You can view his swing trading chart lessons weekly on YouTube.

Mondays, Wednesdays, and Fridays at 10:00 AM EST.

He loves to learn and loves to teach. His students rave about how easy he makes learning the skill of trading the financial markets.

His God-given assignment is to help people learn how to...

Increase On The Sudden